# Subsequent

Ryan Stoute

Order this book online at www.trafford.com
or email orders@trafford.com

Most Trafford titles are also available at major online book retailers.

 www.trafford.com

**North America & international**
toll-free:  844 688 6899 (USA & Canada)
fax: 812 355 4082

Our mission is to efficiently provide the world's finest, most comprehensive book publishing
service, enabling every author to experience success. To find out how to publish your book,
your way, and have it available worldwide, visit us online at www.trafford.com

Because of the dynamic nature of the Internet, any web addresses or links contained in this book may have changed
since publication and may no longer be valid. The views expressed in this work are solely those of the author and do
not necessarily reflect the views of the publisher, and the publisher hereby disclaims any responsibility for them.

Any people depicted in stock imagery provided by Getty Images are models,
and such images are being used for illustrative purposes only.
Certain stock imagery © Getty Images.

ISBN: 978-1-4669-1701-9 (sc)

ISBN: 978-1-4669-1700-2 (e)

Library of Congress Control Number: 2012902950

Print information available on the last page.

Trafford rev. 02/24/2021

Ryan Stoute has a bachelor's degree in English from the University of Massachusetts in Boston and currently lives in Chelsea, Massachusetts.

…ed in the United States

…aker & Taylor Publisher Services